THE CURSE OF
KING TUT'S
TOMB

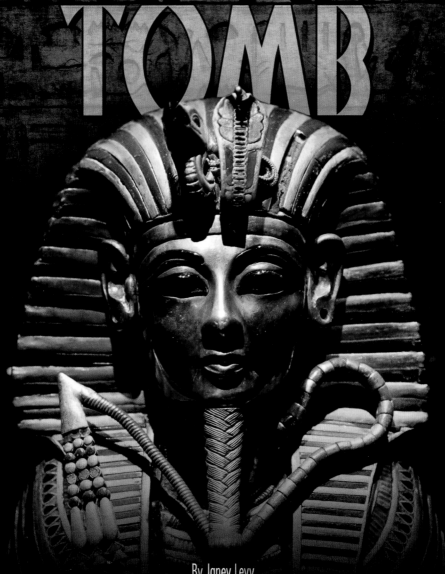

By Janey Levy

Gareth Stevens
PUBLISHING

Please visit our website, www.garethstevens.com. For a free color catalog of all our high-quality books, call toll free 1-800-542-2595 or fax 1-877-542-2596.

Library of Congress Cataloging-in-Publication Data

Levy, Janey, author.
The curse of King Tut's tomb / Janey Levy.
    pages cm. — (History's mysteries)
ISBN 978-1-4824-2082-1 (pbk.)
ISBN 978-1-4824-2081-4 (6 pack)
ISBN 978-1-4824-2083-8 (library binding)
1. Tutankhamen, King of Egypt—Tomb—Juvenile literature. 2. Excavations (Archaeology)—Egypt—Valley of the Kings—Juvenile literature. 3. Egypt—Antiquities—Juvenile literature. 4. Carter, Howard, 1874-1939—Juvenile literature. I. Title. II. Series: History's mysteries (New York, N.Y.)
  DT87.5.L48 2015
  932.014—dc23

2014020527

First Edition

Published in 2015 by
Gareth Stevens Publishing
111 East 14th Street, Suite 349
New York, NY 10003

Designer: Katelyn E. Reynolds
Editor: Therese Shea

Photo credits: Cover, p. 1 Ethan Miller/Getty Images; cover, pp. 1–32 (background texture) Kamira/Shutterstock.com; p. 5 A. Dagli Orti/De Agnostini/Getty Images; p. 7 Hisham Ibrahim/Photographer's Choice/Getty Images; pp. 8, 17 De Agostini Picture Library/Getty Images; p. 9 G. Sioen/De Agostini/Getty Images; pp. 11, 12, 13, 24, 26 Hulton Archive/Getty Images; p. 15 Stringer/Hulton Archive/Getty Images; p. 18 Kenneth Garrett/National Geographic/Getty Images; p. 19 Print Collector/Hulton Archive/Getty Images; p. 21 Mikael Damkier/Shutterstock.com; p. 23 Leemage/Universal Images Group/Getty Images; p. 25 Popperfoto/Getty Images; p. 29 (movie still) Stringer/Hulton Archive/Moviepix/Getty Images; p. 29 (DVD) Universal Studios/Getty Images.

Printed in the United States of America

CPSIA compliance information: Batch #CW15GS: For further information contact Gareth Stevens, New York, New York at 1-800-542-2595.

CONTENTS

Golden Treasure and a Pharaoh's Curse..........4

Egypt's Boy King 6

Seekers of the Lost Tomb 10

Under the Debris, a Tomb 14

"Wonderful Things" 16

Sudden Death..20

Newspapers Claim Killer Curse 22

The Legend Endures 28

Glossary..30

For More Information 31

Index...32

Words in the glossary appear in **bold** type
the first time they are used in the text.

GOLDEN TREASURE
AND A PHARAOH'S CURSE

Gold! Howard Carter saw it gleaming when he peered through a small hole into a dark chamber in November 1922. He had found the ancient Egyptian **pharaoh** Tutankhamun's tomb—and it was nearly untouched. News spread quickly, and people around the world eagerly read newspaper accounts of the discovery.

Yet the story had a dark side. The British noble who funded the **excavation** died shortly after the discovery, prompting rumors of a curse. The tomb reportedly bore a terrible warning: "Death comes on wings to he who enters the tomb of a pharaoh." Additional deaths seemed to confirm the curse. But did the tomb really have such a warning? And could a curse really be killing people? Let's start where the story begins—with Tutankhamun.

REVEALED!

The first ghost story about a mummy's curse was published in 1699.

THE VALLEY OF THE KINGS

By Tutankhamun's time, pharaohs were no longer buried in pyramids. Earlier pyramids had been robbed of their treasures, which pharaohs wanted for the **afterlife**. So pharaohs tried to hide their tombs better. They chose a valley far south of the pyramids and had their tombs cut into the cliffs. This valley is known today as the Valley of the Kings. However, the tombs there weren't any safer from robbers than the pyramids were.

This illustration from a 1923 newspaper shows an artist's idea of what it looked like around Tutankhamun's tomb as treasures were removed to the thrill of gathered crowds.

EGYPT'S
BOY KING

Tutankhamun—often called King Tut—is
rhaps Egypt's most famous pharaoh. But that
me rests on his tomb's riches, not on a long
gn or great accomplishments. He ruled for just
years and is sometimes called the boy king
cause of his youth. He was about 9 when he
came pharaoh and 19 when he died around
24 BC.

Tutankhamun was the son of the pharaoh
henaten, who was famous for his changes
Egyptian religion. Egyptians traditionally
rshipped many gods, but Akhenaten abolished
at practice. He demanded Egyptians worship
ly the sun god, Aten, and tried to erase all
ention of the creator god, Amun. He also
andoned Egypt's capital at Thebes and built a
w one called Amarna.
ese changes upset
any Egyptians.

REVEALED!

Tutankhamun was tall but not strong.
He's the only pharaoh known to have
been shown seated while engaged in
physical activities such as archery.

TUTANKHAMUN'S MOTHER

It was usual in ancient Egypt for pharaohs to have several wives. Akhenaten's chief wife was Nefertiti, but, according to a recent **DNA** study, Tutankhamun's mother was one of Akhenaten's other wives. The study identified her mummy, but her name isn't known. The study also showed she was Akhenaten's sister as well as his wife. This, too, was common practice among ancient Egyptian royalty. It kept power within the royal family.

This scene from the throne found in Tutankhamun's tomb shows the pharaoh with his chief wife, Ankhensenamun, who was also his half sister.

Akhenaten died around 1335 BC, and his young son Tutankhaten soon became pharaoh. The ending of the boy's name, like his father's, reflected devotion to Aten. But Tutankhaten reversed his father's religious reforms. Worship of many gods was restored. Amun became the chief god again, and Tutankhaten changed his name to Tutankhamun to reflect that. Amarna was abandoned, and Thebes became the capital again.

When Tutankhamun died unexpectedly, he was buried hastily in a small tomb. Later pharaohs, who viewed Akhenaten as a **heretic** and tried to erase him from history, chose to ignore the reign of his son Tutankhamun. They allowed the entrance to Tutankhamun's tomb to become covered with debris. In time, everyone—including tomb robbers—forgot Tutankhamun and his tomb.

REVEALED!

Tutankhamun's mummy seems to have burned after it was sealed in its coffin! Scientists think a chemical reaction caused by the oils used to prepare his mummy started the fire.

carving of Akhenaten (left), his wife, and children

Nobody is sure what killed Tutankhamun. Studies of his mummy found he had an **infected** broken leg, and it might have played a role. The recent DNA study that identified his mother also revealed he had suffered several malaria infections. Malaria is a blood disease carried by mosquitoes. That might have contributed to his death, too. The study also showed he had a painful bone disease that would have required him to use a cane.

Today, this is all that remains of Akhenaten's splendid capital city of Amarna.

SEEKERS
OF THE LOST TOMB

British archaeologist Howard Carter began his work in Egypt in 1891 at the age of 17. He started out as an artist whose job was to make drawings of tomb scenes and **inscriptions**. The next year, he began to learn excavation procedures by working for a famous British archaeologist named Flinders Petrie. By 1899, Carter was so well known and well respected that he was appointed inspector for the Egyptian **antiquities** department. He was only 25 years old.

Carter resigned from the antiquities department in 1905 after a disagreement. The next couple of years were difficult, as he looked for jobs with other archaeologists. Things changed around 1907 when Carter met the Earl of Carnarvon. Soon, he was supervising Lord Carnarvon's excavations in Egypt.

REVEALED!

During the time Howard Carter worked in Egypt, the country was controlled by Great Britain.

CARTER AND THE FEMALE PHARAOH

Long before he uncovered Tutankhamun's tomb, Carter found the tomb of the famous Egyptian queen Hatshepsut. She was the chief wife of Thutmose II. When Thutmose died, Hatshepsut stole the throne from his son and proclaimed herself pharaoh. She even had herself shown in artworks as a man! She ruled from 1473 BC to 1458 BC and was the first pharaoh to build a tomb in the Valley of the Kings.

This picture shows Howard Carter in the 1920s, after he had gained fame for his discovery of Tutankhamun's tomb.

George Herbert, the Earl of Carnarvon, was just another wealthy British lord when he was injured in an automobile accident in 1901. The accident left him in poor health, and in 1903, he began spending winters in Egypt to escape England's cold, damp weather. He took up archaeology as a hobby, and, like many wealthy English and American citizens, funded excavations in Egypt.

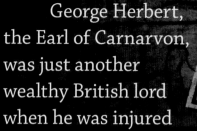

REVEALED!

Many archaeologists believed there was nothing left to find in the Valley of the Kings, but Carter continued his search for Tutankhamun's tomb there anyway.

By the spring of 1922, Carter and Lord Carnarvon had spent about 7 years searching for Tutankhamun's tomb in the Valley of the Kings. Lord Carnarvon was ready to give up and start excavations somewhere else in Egypt. Carter talked him into funding one more season. Neither man realized then how close they were to success.

Lord Carnarvon

CLUES AMONG THE SCRAPS

Why did Carter believe Tutankhamun's tomb was in the Valley of the Kings? He recognized important clues in material discovered earlier in the valley. Another British archaeologist had found a pit containing gigantic pottery jars filled with broken mud seals, torn linen strips, and other material that seemed worthless. But Tutankhamun's name appeared on some of the material. Carter realized the material was left over from Tutankhamun's burial—and that meant the tomb must be nearby.

This 1922 photograph shows Lord Carnarvon (in the center walking with a cane) inspecting an Egyptian tomb.

UNDER THE DEBRIS, A TOMB

On November 1, 1922, Carter began excavating a spot located below the tomb of Rameses VI and across from the pit that held Tutankhamun's burial leftovers. On November 4, the workers uncovered a step cut into the rock. A day later, they'd uncovered 12 steps and the upper part of a door. It was a tomb entrance! The intact seals on the door suggested thieves hadn't robbed the tomb. But the visible seals didn't tell who was buried inside.

The workers re-covered the steps to hide the find, while Carter sent a telegram to Lord Carnarvon in England. On November 24, after Lord Carnarvon's arrival, the workers cleared all 16 steps and revealed the full door. Seals at the bottom bore Tutankhamun's name. They'd found his tomb!

REVEALED!

Carter's telegram to Lord Carnarvon read: "At last have made wonderful discovery in Valley; a magnificent tomb with seals intact; re-covered same for your arrival; congratulations."

SIGNS OF ANCIENT ROBBERS

When the door was revealed, Carter realized ancient tomb robbers had broken through the upper left. But the door had been resealed, which wouldn't have been done if robbers had emptied the tomb. After the door was removed, Carter could tell robbers had created a small tunnel through the rock fill in the passage beyond. Such material was put into tomb passages to block robbers. At Tutankhamun's tomb, it prevented them from removing large items.

This photograph from around 1925 shows an Egyptian worker standing guard in the passage inside Tutankhamun's tomb. Behind him are the stairs leading to the surface whose discovery by Carter in November 1922 created such excitement.

"WONDERFUL THINGS"

The rock-filled passage beyond the door was 26 feet (8 m) long. By the afternoon of November 26, workers had removed the rock fill, revealing another sealed door. Carter made a small hole in the upper left corner and poked a rod through. The rod struck nothing, which meant the space beyond wasn't filled with rock. Carter enlarged the hole, stuck a lighted candle through, and peered inside. His eyes slowly adjusted to the dim light.

Finally, Lord Carnarvon asked, "Can you see anything?" Carter replied, "Yes, wonderful things." The chamber was filled with all sorts of objects, and everywhere gold gleamed in the candlelight. They had found Tutankhamun's tomb, and it was nearly whole. They had uncovered the greatest collection of Egyptian antiquities ever discovered.

REVEALED!

Carter wrote about his feelings when he saw what was in the chamber: "For the moment—an eternity it must have seemed to the others standing by—I was struck dumb with amazement."

Why did Egyptians put so many objects in tombs? Everything was meant to serve the dead person in the afterlife. Life on Earth was short—most Egyptians died by the age of 40—but the afterlife was forever, so people wanted to have the best things they could. Tombs contained clothes, jewelry, makeup, furniture, food, and drink. Even the mummy was necessary. In Egyptian religion, the soul needed the body in the afterlife.

These are just a few of the spectacular treasures found in Tutankhamun's tomb.

Tutankhamun's tomb had four chambers, each filled with treasure. The first chamber Carter and Lord Carnarvon entered is known as the Antechamber. A small room off the back of it is called the Annex. The Burial Chamber and the Treasure Chamber are off one side of the Antechamber.

Work on the tomb progressed slowly. Each object had to be photographed and recorded before it could be removed. Many objects were in delicate condition and had to be carefully wrapped for protection. Carter and Lord Carnarvon finally entered the Burial Chamber on February 17, 1923, after weeks spent removing objects from the Antechamber. It was a year and a half before Tutankhamun's coffin was opened. Carter didn't finish his work on the tomb until 1932.

REVEALED!

News of the discovery had brought hundreds of tourists and reporters to the tomb. They waited around the entrance for a glimpse of the tomb's treasures as the objects were removed.

gold coffin of Tutankhamun

Painted funeral scenes coated the Burial Chamber's walls. A huge shrine made of wood covered with gold almost completely filled the room. It contained another shrine, which contained another, which surrounded yet another. Inside the fourth shrine was Tutankhamun's stone **sarcophagus**. It contained a wooden coffin covered with gold, which held a second coffin. Inside the second coffin was the third and final coffin. It was solid gold and held Tutankhamun's mummy!

Scenes of human and animal figures against a gold background decorate the walls of the Burial Chamber around Tutankhamun's stone sarcophagus.

SUDDEN DEATH

Because of his poor health, Lord Carnarvon was exhausted by the excitement accompanying the opening of the Burial Chamber. So he left the Valley of the Kings on February 28, 1923, and went to Aswan to rest. Around this time, a mosquito bit him on the cheek. Such an event isn't necessarily serious. Mosquito bites are common occurrences. But Lord Carnarvon's mosquito bite became infected, and he became ill. His illness was so serious it was decided to move him to Cairo, where his personal doctor from England would meet him. But in Cairo, Lord Carnarvon became even sicker and died on April 5.

Rumors of a curse immediately appeared in newspapers. They were partly a result of a situation Lord Carnarvon himself had created.

REVEALED!

Mosquitoes may also have contributed to Tutankhamun's death, since they were the source of his many malaria infections.

HOW A MOSQUITO KILLED LORD CARNARVON

How did a mosquito bite become so seriously infected it killed someone? The infection began after Lord Carnarvon cut the bite while shaving. That led to blood poisoning and then pneumonia, a serious lung disease. This series of events likely wouldn't happen to everyone. But remember, Lord Carnarvon was in poor health already. His body lacked the strength to fight infection.

The Cairo Lord Carnarvon was taken to would have looked much like this: a crowded city with dusty streets.

NEWSPAPERS CLAIM
KILLER CURSE

Ancient Egypt had long fascinated Europeans and Americans. The discovery of Tutankhamun's tomb whipped the fascination into wild excitement. People demanded daily updates on happenings at the tomb, and newspapers were eager to provide them. But Lord Carnarvon and Carter didn't want crowds to interfere with work. Lord Carnarvon thought the solution was to give **exclusive** rights to the *Times*, the major newspaper in London, England. That way, Lord Carnarvon and Carter would only have to deal with one newspaper.

The solution didn't work as planned. Other newspapers simply made up stories. And the stories often included curses threatening death to those who entered the tomb—even though there was NO CURSE anywhere on the tomb. The stories were especially common after Lord Carnarvon became ill.

REVEALED!

Why did newspapers publish made-up stories about curses? The reason is simple: The stories were popular with the public and sold newspapers.

FICTIONAL PHARAOH'S CURSES

Different accounts of the curse on Tutankhamun's tomb appeared. One newspaper reported it said, "They who enter this sacred tomb shall swift be visited by wings of death." Another newspaper took a real inscription from a statue of Anubis, the Egyptian god who led souls to judgment, and added the following curse to it: "I will kill all those who cross this **threshold** into the sacred **precincts** of the Royal King who lives forever."

Le Petit Journal illustré

PARAISSANT LE DIMANCHE

34e Année - N° 1677

This illustration comes from the front page of a French newspaper published in February 1923. It shows what an artist imagined the scene looked like when Carter and Lord Carnarvon first entered Tutankhamun's tomb.

Statements by famous people fueled belief in curses. After Lord Carnarvon became ill, best-selling British writer Marie Corelli wrote she had an ancient book that claimed horrible punishment awaited anyone who entered a sealed tomb. She added, "That is why I ask, Was it a mosquito bite that has so seriously infected Lord Carnarvon?" When Lord Carnarvon died a few days later, it appeared she was correct.

Even celebrated writer Arthur Conan Doyle credited the idea of a curse. Doyle is known for creating the famously logical fictional detective Sherlock Holmes. But after Lord Carnarvon died, Doyle wrote, "Powerful elementals or spirits placed on guard by ancient Egyptian priests to protect the tomb of King Tutankhamun may have caused the death of Lord Carnarvon."

REVEALED!

Some people suggested Lord Carnarvon's death was really caused by a poison he was exposed to in Tutankhamun's tomb.

the excavation team including Howard Carter (fourth from right) and Lord Carnarvon (third from right)

"SUPERSTITION AROUSED"

A newspaper article written the day after Lord Carnarvon's death noted events that superstitious people pointed to as "proof" of a curse. It was said the lights in Lord Carnarvon's room went out twice at the time of his death. It was also reported that his personal doctor didn't arrive from England in time because his boat was late, causing him to miss the train to Cairo.

Howard Carter, left, and Lord Carnarvon pose next to the partly torn-down wall between the Antechamber and the Burial Chamber.

Soon rumors were flying of more deaths linked to the tomb's curse.

Reportedly Lord Carnarvon's dog, far away in England, let out a great howl and died at the exact moment of her master's death. Another story said a cobra—a common symbol for pharaohs in ancient Egypt—killed Carter's pet canary on the day the tomb was opened. Four people who visited the tomb soon after it was opened really did die the following year, and their deaths were blamed on the curse.

To some people, Lord Carnarvon's death and the others prove the curse is real. But a closer examination of the facts reveals more ordinary explanations. The chart on the next page lists some deaths blamed on the curse and the actual facts surrounding them.

carrying crates out of Tut's tomb

COULD AN ANCIENT TOMB REALLY MAKE YOU SICK?

Has modern science found anything in ancient tombs that could make you sick?
Some studies have shown ancient tombs may contain bacteria that attack the lungs.
Coffins may contain chemicals that can harm the lungs. The food offerings left in
the tomb might grow molds that can infect the lungs or cause deadly diseases.
However, experts don't believe anything that might have been in Tutankhamun's
tomb contributed to Lord Carnarvon's death.

DEATH FACTS

DEATH	FACTS
Lord Carnarvon	Had been in poor health for over 20 years. Suffered a serious infection and didn't immediately receive medical care.
Lord Carnarvon's dog died at exact moment of her master's death.	Although the dog did die, the account of the time and manner of her death isn't considered reliable.
Howard Carter's pet canary killed by cobra on day tomb was opened.	Not certain that the canary died or was attacked by a cobra.
Prince Ali Kahmel Falim Bey visited the newly opened tomb and died shortly after.	The prince was killed by his wife.
Colonel Aubrey Herbert visited the newly opened tomb and died shortly after.	Died from problems related to a dental procedure that wasn't done properly.
George Jay Gould visited the newly opened tomb and died shortly after.	Died from an illness.
Woolf Joel visited the newly opened tomb and died shortly after.	Died from a gunshot wound.

THE LEGEND ENDURES

Thrilling tales of ancient tombs, mummies, and curses capture the imagination, so the legend of Tutankhamun's curse endures. As late as the 1970s—50 years after the tomb's discovery—deaths were blamed on the curse, including members of the crew on the airplane that carried Tutankhamun's treasures to London for a 1972 museum exhibit.

The curse's continuing popularity has prompted many people to write articles and books disproving it. A German archaeologist wrote a booklet in 1933. In his 1997 book *Encyclopedia of Claims, Frauds, and Hoaxes of the Occult and Supernatural*, famous magician James Randi demonstrated that people present at the opening of the tomb actually lived longer than normal. There are recent articles disproving the curse as well. Yet some still believe. Do you?

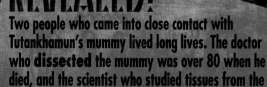

REVEALED!

Two people who came into close contact with Tutankhamun's mummy lived long lives. The doctor who **dissected** the mummy was over 80 when he died, and the scientist who studied tissues from the mummy died at 79.

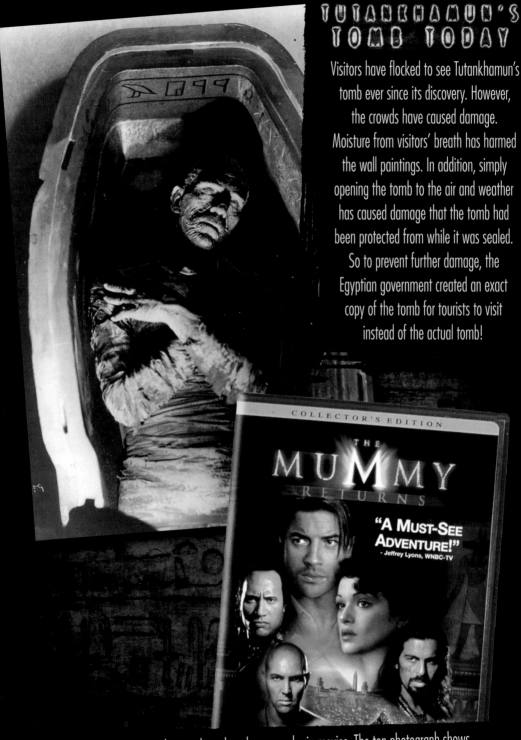

TUTANKHAMUN'S TOMB TODAY

Visitors have flocked to see Tutankhamun's tomb ever since its discovery. However, the crowds have caused damage. Moisture from visitors' breath has harmed the wall paintings. In addition, simply opening the tomb to the air and weather has caused damage that the tomb had been protected from while it was sealed. So to prevent further damage, the Egyptian government created an exact copy of the tomb for tourists to visit instead of the actual tomb!

Tales of mummies and curses have long been popular in movies. The top photograph shows Boris Karloff as an evil mummy in his sarcophagus in the 1932 movie *The Mummy*. The bottom photograph shows the cover of a DVD of the blockbuster 2001 movie *The Mummy Returns*.

GLOSSARY

afterlife: an existence after death

antiquities: objects or monuments of ancient times

dissect: to cut open a dead body to study it for scientific purposes

DNA: a molecule in the body that carries genetic information, which gives the instructions for life

excavation: the act or process of digging and removing earth in order to find something

exclusive: limiting possession, control, or use to a single person or group

heretic: one who does not follow established or accepted religious beliefs

infect: to introduce a disease-causing substance

inscription: something that is written

pharaoh: a ruler of ancient Egypt

precinct: an enclosed space bounded by the walls of a building

sarcophagus: a stone coffin

threshold: an entrance or doorway

INFORMATION

BOOKS

Edwards, Roberta. *Who Was King Tut?* New York, NY: Grosset & Dunlap, 2006.

Hyde, Natalie. *King Tut.* New York, NY: Crabtree Publishing, 2014.

Zoehfeld, Kathleen Weidner. *The Curse of King Tut's Mummy.* New York, NY: Random House Children's Books, 2007.

WEBSITES

Explore King Tut's Tomb
www.pbs.org/wnet/pharaohs/tut.html
Examine the treasures found in King Tut's tomb on this interactive website.

Howard Carter and the Curse of Tut's Mummy
www.unmuseum.org/mummy.htm
Read more about the discovery of King Tut's tomb and the supposed curse, see photos of Howard Carter in the tomb, and watch a video.

The Story of King Tut
archive.fieldmuseum.org/tut/interactive/Tut_content.html
Explore King Tut's tomb as well as other tombs in the Valley of the Kings, and see historical photos on this interactive website.

INDEX

afterlife 5, 17

Akhenaten 6, 7, 8, 9

Amarna 6, 8, 9

Ankhensenamun 7

Annex 18

Antechamber 18, 25

antiquities 10, 16

Burial Chamber 18, 19,
    20, 25

burial materials 13, 14

Cairo 20, 21, 25, 26

Carter, Howard 4, 10, 11,
    12, 13, 14, 15, 16,
    18, 22, 23, 24, 25

Carter's pet canary 26,
    27

coffin 8, 18, 19, 27

Corelli, Marie 24

DNA study 7, 9

Doyle, Arthur Conan 24

gold 4, 16, 18, 19

Lord Carnarvon 10, 12,
    13, 14, 16, 18, 20,
    21, 22, 23, 24, 25,
    26, 27

Lord Carnarvon's dog 26,
    27

made-up stories 22

mosquito bite 20, 21, 24

movies 29

mummy 4, 7, 8, 9, 17, 19,
    28, 29

newspapers 4, 5, 20, 22,
    23, 25

religion 6, 8, 17

rumors 4, 20, 26

sarcophagus 19, 29

Thebes 6, 8

Times 22

tomb robbers 5, 8, 14, 15

Treasure Chamber 18

treasures 5, 17, 18, 28

Valley of the Kings 5, 11,
    12, 13, 20